NINJA FOODI

BY CHOA SUI

CONTENTS

Chapter 1: Breakfast

Lovely Butter Pancakes

(Prepping time: 5 minutes\ Cooking time: 10 minutes | For 4 servings)

Ingredients

- 2 cups cream cheese
- 2 cups almond flour
- 6 large whole eggs
- 1/4 teaspoon salt
- 2 tablespoons butter
- ¼ teaspoon ground ginger
- ½ teaspoon cinnamon powder

Directions

1. Take a large bowl and add cream cheese, eggs, 1 tablespoon butter. Blend on high until creamy

2. Slow add flour and keep beating

3. Add salt, ginger, cinnamon

4. Keep beating until fully mixed

5. Set your Ninja Foodi to Saute mode and grease stainless steel insert Add butter and heat it up

6. Add ½ cup batter and cook for 2-3 minutes, flip and cook the other side

7. Repeat with the remaining batter, Enjoy!

Nutrition Values (Per Serving)

- Calories: 432
- Fat: 40g
- Carbohydrates: 3g
- Protein: 14g
- Sodium: 334g
- Fiber: 1g
- Saturated Fat: 8g

Cheesy Mushroom Hats

(Prepping time: 10 minutes\ Cooking time: 6 minutes |For 3 servings)

Ingredients

- 10 ounces mushroom hats
- 2 ounces parmesan, grated
- ½ teaspoon oregano, dried
- 1-ounce fresh parsley, chopped
- 1-ounce cheddar cheese, grated
- 2 tablespoons cream cheese
- ½ teaspoon chili flakes

Directions

1. Mix together the chopped pars0ley, cream cheese, chili flakes, grated cheese, and dried oregano

2. Fill up the mushroom hats with the cheese mixture

3. Place the mushroom hats in the rack

4. Lower the air fryer lid

5. Cook the meat for 6 minutes at 400 F

6. Then check the mushroom cooked or not if you want you can cook for 2-3 minutes more

7. Serve hot and enjoy!

Nutrition Values (Per Serving)

- Calories: 147

- Fat: 9.9g

- Carbohydrates: 4.9g

- Protein: 12.8g

- Sodium: 365g

- Fiber: 2g

- Saturated Fat: 3g

Lovely Egg Salad

(Prepping time: 5 minutes\ Cooking time: 15 minutes |For 2 servings)

Ingredients

- 3 eggs
- 1 teaspoon olive oil
- ½ white onion, sliced
- 1 avocado, chopped
- 3 tablespoons heavy cream
- ½ teaspoon paprika
- ½ teaspoon salt

Directions

1. Take a trivet and place the eggs into it

2. Lower the air fryer lid

3. Cook the eggs for 15 minutes at 270 F

4. In between, combine heavy cream, salt, chopped avocado, onion, and paprika

5. Once cooked, let the chill in the icy water and then peel them

6. Cut the eggs into quarters and add in the avocado mixture

7. Then stir the salad

8. Serve and enjoy!

Nutrition Values (Per Serving)

- Calories: 410

- Fat: 36.2g

- Carbohydrates: 12.2g

- Protein: 11.4g

- Sodium: 194g

- Fiber: 4g

- Saturated Fat: 3g

Western Omelet

Prep Time: 10 minutes

Cooking Time: 30-35 minutes

Number of Servings: 4

Ingredients:

- 3 eggs, whisked
- 3 ounces chorizo, chopped
- 1-ounces Feta cheese, crumbled
- 5 tablespoons almond milk
- ¾ teaspoon chili flakes
- ¼ teaspoon salt
- 1 green pepper, chopped

Method:

1. Add listed ingredients to To a bowl and mix well

2. Take an omelet pan and pour the mixture on it

3. Pre-heat your Ninja Food on "BAKE" mode, at a temperature of 320 degrees F

4. Transfer pan with omelet mix to your Ninja Foodi and cook for 30 minutes, or until the surface is golden and the egg has set properly

5. Serve and enjoy!

Nutritional Values (Per Serving)

- Calories: 426
- Fat: 38g
- Saturated Fat: 5 g
- Carbohydrates: 7 g
- Fiber: 2 g
- Sodium: 803 mg
- Protein: 21 g

Lovely Egg Devils

Prep Time: 10 minutes

Cooking Time: 10 minutes

Number of Servings: 4

Ingredients:

- 8 large eggs
- 1 cup of water
- Guacamole
- Sliced Radishes
- Mayonnaise
- Furikake

Method:

1. Add water to the inner pot of your Ninja Foodi
2. Place the steamer rack inside the pot and arrange the eggs on top of the rack
3. Lock pressure lid and cook on HIGH pressure for 6 minutes
4. Release pressure naturally over 10 minutes and transfer the eggs to a bowl full of icy water
5. Peel after 5 minutes
6. Cut in half and decorate with guacamole, sliced radish, mayo and enjoy!

Nutritional Values (Per Serving)

- Calories: 70
- Fat: 6g
- Saturated Fat: 1 g
- Carbohydrates: 1 g
- Fiber: 0.5 g
- Sodium: 684 mg
- Protein: 3 g

Decisive Ham And Eggs Casserole

Prep Time: 10 minutes

Cooking Time: 5 minutes

Number of Servings: 4

Ingredients:

- 4 whole eggs
- 1 tablespoons milk
- 1 tomato, diced
- ½ cup spinach
- ¼ teaspoon salt
- ¼ teaspoon ground black pepper

Method:

1. Take a baking pan (small enough to fit Ninja Foodi) and grease it with butter

2. Take a medium bowl and whisk in eggs, milk, salt, pepper, add veggies to the bowl and stir

3. Pour egg mixture into the baking pan and lower the pan into the Ninja Foodi

4. Close Air Crisping lid and Air Crisp for 325 degrees for 7 minutes

5. Remove the pan from eggs and enjoy hot!

Nutritional Values (Per Serving)

- Calories: 78
- Fat: 5g
- Saturated Fat: 2 g
- Carbohydrates: 1 g
- Fiber: 0.1 g
- Sodium:638 mg
- Protein: 7 g

Awesome Broccoli Florets

Prep Time: 10 minutes

Cooking Time: 6 minutes

Number of Servings: 4

Ingredients:

- 4 tablespoons butter, melted
- Salt and pepper to taste
- 2 pounds broccoli florets
- 1 cup whipping cream

Method:

1. Place a steamer basket in your Ninja Foodi (bottom part) and add water
2. Place florets on top of the basket and lock lid
3. Cook on HIGH pressure for 5 minutes
4. Quick-release pressure
5. Transfer florets from the steamer basket to the pot
6. Add salt, pepper, butter, and stir
7. Lock crisping lid and cook on Air Crisp mode for 360 degrees F
8. Serve and enjoy!

Nutritional Values (Per Serving)

- Calories: 178
- Fat: 14g
- Saturated Fat: 4 g
- Carbohydrates: 8 g
- Fiber: 2 g
- Sodium: 180 mg
- Protein: 5g

Nut Packed Porridge Dish

Prep Time: 10 minutes

Cooking Time: 10 minutes

Number of Servings: 6

Ingredients:

- 1 cup pecans, halved
- 1 cup cashew nuts, raw and unsalted
- 4 teaspoons coconut oil, melted
- 2 cups of water

Method:

1. Add 1 and ½ cups water and place a steamer rack in your Ninja Foodi

2. Trim the core of the cauliflower head and cut into florets

3. Take a small bowl and mix with olive oil, salt, cumin, and paprika, then drizzle over cauliflower

4. Close the lid

5. Cook for 4 minutes on High

6. Quick-release the pressure

7. Garnish with cilantro

8. Serve and enjoy!

Nutritional Values (Per Serving)

- Calories: 70
- Fat: 6g
- Saturated Fat: g
- Carbohydrates: 1 g
- Fiber: 0 g
- Sodium: 79 mg
- Protein: 3g

Chapter 2: Vegetarian And Vegan Recipes

Creamy Mushroom Soup

(Prepping time: 10 minutes\ Cooking time: 10 minutes |For 6 servings)

Ingredients

- 1 small onion, diced
- 8 ounces white button mushrooms, chopped
- 8 ounces portabella mushrooms
- 2 garlic cloves, minced
- ¼ cup dry white wine vinegar
- 2 and ½ cup mushroom stock
- 2 teaspoons salt
- 1 teaspoon fresh thyme
- ¼ teaspoon black pepper

Cashew Cream

- 1/3 cup of raw cashew
- ½ a cup of mushroom stock

Directions

1. Add onion, mushroom to the pot and set your Ninja Foodi to Saute mode

2. Cook for 8 minutes and stir from time to time

3. Add garlic and Saute for 2 minutes more

4. Add wine and Saute until evaporated

5. Add thyme, pepper, salt, Mushroom stock, and stir

6. Lock up the lid and cook on HIGH pressure for 5 minutes

7. Perform quick release

8. Transfer cashew and water to the blender and blend well

9. Remove lid and transfer the mix to the blender

10. Blend until smooth

11. Server and enjoy!

Nutrition Values (Per Serving)

- Calories: 193
- Fats: 12g
- Carbs:15g
- Protein: 5
- Sodium: 232g
- Fiber: 2g
- Saturated Fat: 3g

Creative Coconut Cabbage

(Prepping time: 10 minutes \ Cooking time: 7 minutes |For 4 servings)

Ingredients

- 2 tablespoons lemon juice
- 1/3 medium carrot, sliced
- ½ ounces, yellow onion, sliced
- 1/2 cup cabbage, shredded
- 1 teaspoon turmeric powder
- 1 ounce dry coconut
- ½ tablespoon mustard powder
- ½ teaspoon mild curry powder
- 1 large garlic cloves, diced
- 1 and ½ teaspoons salt
- 1/3 cup water
- 3 tablespoons olive oil
- 3 large whole eggs
- 3 large egg yolks

Directions

1. Set your Ninja Foodi to Saute mode and add oil, stir in onions, salt and cook for 4 minutes

2. Stir in spices, garlic and Saute for 30 seconds

3. Stir in rest of the ingredients, lock lid, and cook on HIGH pressure for 3 minutes

4. Naturally, release the pressure over 10 minutes

5. Serve and enjoy!

<u>Nutrition Values (Per Serving)</u>

- Calories: 400
- Fat: 34g
- Carbohydrates: 10g
- Protein: 14g
- Sodium: 268g
- Fiber: 3g
- Saturated Fat: 7g

Juicy Spaghetti Squash Zoodles

(Prepping time: 10 minutes\ Cooking time: 7 minutes |For 6 servings)

Ingredients

- 2 pound of spaghetti squash
- 1 cup of water

Directions

1. Take a paring knife and cut the spaghetti squash in half

2. Take a largely sized spoon and scoop out the center seeds and discard the gunk

3. Place the Ninja Foodi steamer insert inside the inner pot of your Ninja Foodi

4. Add 1 cup of water

5. Add the half-cut squashes to the steamer insert, making sure that the cut part if facing up

6. Lock up the lid and cook on HIGH pressure for 7 minutes

7. Once done, perform a quick release

8. Take the squash out and fork out the strings

9. Serve with sauce or your favorite topping!

Nutrition Values (Per Serving)

- Calories: 45
- Fats: 5g
- Carbs:7g

- Protein:3g
- Sodium: 686g
- Fiber: 3g
- Saturated Fat: 2g

Breezy Fresh Onion Soup

Prep Time: 10 minutes

Cooking Time: 10-15 minutes

Number of Servings: 4

Ingredients:

- 2 tablespoons avocado oil
- 8 cups yellow onion
- 1 tablespoon balsamic vinegar
- 6 cups of pork stock
- 1 teaspoon salt
- 2 bay leaves
- 2 large sprigs, fresh thyme

Method:

1. Cut the onion in half through the root
2. Peel and slice them into half-moons
3. Set your Ninja Foodi to Saute mode and add oil, let the oil heat up
4. Add onions, cook for 5 minutes
5. Add vinegar, scrape any frond from bottom
6. Add stock, leaves, thyme, and stir
7. Lock lid and cook on HIGH pressure for 10 minutes
8. Release the pressure naturally over 10 minutes
9. Discard leaves and thyme stem
10. Take an immersion blender and blend the soup well
11. Serve and enjoy!

Nutritional Values (Per Serving)

- Calories: 454
- Fat: 31g
- Saturated Fat: 5 g
- Carbohydrates: 7 g
- Fiber: 1 g

- Sodium: 445 mg
- Protein: 27 g

Fancy Beet Borscht

Prep Time: 10 minutes

Cooking Time: 45 minutes

Number of Servings: 4

Ingredients:

- 8 cups beets
- ½ cup celery, diced
- ½ cup carrots, diced
- 2 garlic cloves, diced
- 1 medium onion, diced
- 3 cups cabbage, shredded
- 6 cups beef stock
- 1 bay leaf
- 1 tablespoon salt
- ½ tablespoon thyme
- ¼ cup fresh dill, chopped
- ½ cup of coconut yogurt

Method:

1. Add the washed beets to a steamer in the Ninja Foodi
2. Add 1 cup of water
3. Steam for 7 minutes
4. Perform a quick release and drop into an ice bath
5. Carefully peel off the skin and dice the beets
6. Transfer the diced beets, celery, carrots, onion, garlic, cabbage, stock, bay leaf, thyme and salt to your Instant Pot
7. Lock up the lid and set the pot to SOUP mode, cook for 45 minutes
8. Release the pressure naturally
9. Transfer to bowls and top with a dollop of dairy-free yogurt
10. Enjoy with a garnish of fresh dill!

Nutritional Values (Per Serving)

- Calories: 625
- Fat: 46 g
- Saturated Fat: 10 g
- Carbohydrates: 19 g
- Fiber: 2 g
- Sodium: 3331 mg
- Protein: 90 g

Zucchini Pesto Dish

Prep Time: 10 minutes

Cooking Time: 10 minutes

Number of Servings: 4

Ingredients:

- 1 tablespoon olive oil
- 1 onion, chopped
- 2 and ½ pound roughly chopped zucchini
- ½ cup of water
- 1 and ½ teaspoon salt
- 1 bunch basil leaves
- 2 garlic cloves, minced
- 1 tablespoon extra-virgin olive oil
- Zucchini for making zoodles

Method:

1. Set the Ninja Foodi to Saute mode and add olive oil
2. Once the oil is hot, add onion and Saute for 4 minutes
3. Add zucchini, water, and salt
4. Lock up the lid and cook on HIGH pressure for 3 minutes
5. Release the pressure naturally
6. Add basil, garlic, and leaves
7. Use an immersion blender to blend everything well until you have a sauce-like consistency
8. Take the extra zucchini and pass them through a Spiralizer to get noodle-like shapes
9. Toss the Zoodles with sauce and enjoy!

Nutritional Values (Per Serving)

- Calories: 71
- Fat: 4 g
- Saturated Fat: 1 g

- Carbohydrates: 6 g
- Fiber: 1 g
- Sodium: 411 mg
- Protein: 3 g

Simple Fried Eggs

Prep Time: 10 minutes

Cooking Time: 10 minutes

Number of Servings: 4

Ingredients:

- 4 eggs
- ¼ teaspoon ground black pepper
- 1 teaspoon butter, melted
- ¾ teaspoon salt

Method:

1. Take a small egg pan and brush it with butter.
2. Beat the eggs in the pan
3. Sprinkle with the ground black pepper and salt
4. Transfer the egg pan in the pot
5. Lower the air fryer lid
6. Cook the meat for 10 minutes at 350 F
7. Serve immediately and enjoy!

Nutritional Values (Per Serving)

- Calories: 142
- Fat: 10g
- Saturated Fat: 2 g
- Carbohydrates: 0.9 g
- Fiber: 0 g
- Sodium:250 mg
- Protein: 11 g

Sausage And Egg Breakfast

Prep Time: 10 minutes

Cooking Time: 20 minutes

Number of Servings: 4

Ingredients:

- 4 whole eggs
- 4 sausages, cooked and sliced
- 2 tablespoons butter
- ½ cup mozzarella cheese, grated
- ½ cup cream

Method:

1. Take a bowl and mix everything

2. Add egg mix to your Ninja Foodi, top with cheese and sausage slices

3. Lock pressure lid and select "BAKE/ROAST" mode and cook for 20 minutes at 345 degrees F

4. Take it out once done, serve, and enjoy!

Nutritional Values (Per Serving)

- Calories: 180
- Fat: 12g
- Saturated Fat: 2 g
- Carbohydrates: 4 g
- Fiber: 1 g
- Sodium: 261 mg
- Protein: 12 g

Chapter 3: Chicken And Poultry Recipes

Mexican Chicken Soup

(Prepping time: 5 minutes\ Cooking time: 20 minutes |For 4 servings)

Ingredients

- 2 cups chicken, shredded
- 4 tablespoons olive oil
- ½ cup cilantro, chopped
- 8 cups chicken broth
- 1/3 cup salsa
- 1 teaspoon onion powder
- ½ cup scallions, chopped
-
- 4 ounces green chilies, chopped
- ½ teaspoon habanero, minced
- 1 cup celery root, chopped
- 1 teaspoon cumin
- 1 teaspoon garlic powder
- Salt and pepper to taste

Directions

1. Add all ingredients to Ninja Foodi
2. Stir and lock lid, cook on HIGH pressure for 10 minutes
3. Release pressure naturally over 10 minutes
4. Serve and enjoy!

Nutrition Values (Per Serving)

- Calories: 204
- Fat: 14g
- Carbohydrates: 4g
- Protein: 14g
- Sodium: 1736g
- Fiber: 2g
- Saturated Fat: 6g

Chicken Meatballs And Cabbage

*(Prepping time: 10 minutes + 30 minutes\ Cooking time: 4-6 minutes
|For 4 servings)*

Ingredients

- 1 pound ground chicken
- ¼ cup heavy whip cream
- 2 teaspoons salt
- ½ teaspoon ground caraway seeds
- 1 and ½ teaspoons fresh ground black pepper, divided
- 1/4 teaspoon ground allspice
- 4-6 cups green cabbage, thickly chopped
- ½ cup almond milk
- 2 tablespoons unsalted butter

Directions

1. Transfer meat to a bowl and add cream, 1 teaspoon salt, caraway, ½ teaspoon pepper, allspice, and mix it well

2. Let the mixture chill for 30 minutes

3. Once the mixture is ready, use your hands to scoop the mixture into meatballs

4. Add half of your balls to the Ninja Foodi pot and cover with half of the cabbage

5. Add remaining balls and cover with the rest of the cabbage

6. Add milk, pats of butter, season with salt and pepper

7. Lock lid and cook on HIGH pressure for 4 minutes

8. Quick-release pressure

9. Unlock lid and serve

10. Enjoy!

Nutrition Values (Per Serving)

- Calories: 294
- Fat: 26g
- Carbohydrates: 4g
- Protein: 12g
- Sodium: 804g
- Fiber: 1g
- Saturated Fat: 6g

Flavorful Garlic Chicken

Prep Time: 10 minutes

Cooking Time: 30 minutes

Number of Servings: 4

Ingredients:

- 1-2 pounds chicken breast
- 1 teaspoon salt
- 1 onion, diced
- 1 tablespoon ghee
- 5 garlic cloves, minced
- ½ cup organic chicken broth
- 1 teaspoon dried parsley
- 1 large lemon juice
- 3-4 teaspoon arrowroot flour

Method:

1. Set your Ninja Foodi to Saute mode
2. Add diced up the onion and cooking fat
3. Allow the onions to cook for 5 -10 minutes
4. Add the rest of the ingredients except arrowroot flour
5. Lock up the lid and set the pot to poultry mode
6. Cook until the timer runs out
7. Allow the pressure to release naturally
8. Once done, remove ¼ cup of the sauce from the pot and add arrowroot to make a slurry
9. Add the slurry to the pot to make the gravy thick
10. Keep stirring well
11. Serve!

Nutritional Values (Per Serving)

- Calories: 462
- Fat: 60g
- Saturated Fat: 12 g

- Carbohydrates: 5 g
- Fiber: 2 g
- Sodium: 382 mg
- Protein: 51 g

Mushroom And Chicken Delish

Prep Time: 10 minutes

Cooking Time: 25 minutes

Number of Servings: 4

Ingredients:

- 1 and ½ cups unsweetened coconut milk
- 1 pound chicken thigh, skinless
- 3-4 garlic cloves, crushed
- ½ an onion, finely diced
- 2-inch knob ginger, minced
- 1 cup mushrooms, sliced
- 4 ounces baby spinach
- ½ teaspoon of cayenne pepper
- ½ teaspoon turmeric
- 1 teaspoon salt
- 1 teaspoon Garam Masala
- ¼ cup cilantro, chopped

Method:

1. Add the listed ingredients to your Ninja Foodi

2. Lock lid and cook on HIGH pressure for 15 minutes

3. Release pressure naturally over 10 minutes

4. Remove chicken and roughly puree the veggies using an immersion blender

5. Shred chicken and add it back to the pot

6. Add cream and stir

7. Serve and enjoy!

Nutritional Values (Per Serving)

- Calories: 289
- Fat: 18g
- Saturated Fat: 2 g

- Carbohydrates: 5 g
- Fiber: 2 g
- Sodium: 330 mg
- Protein: 14 g

Summer Chicken Salad

Prep Time: 10 minutes

Cooking Time: 10 minutes

Number of Servings: 4

Ingredients:

- 8 boneless chicken thighs
- Kosher salt
- 1 tablespoon of ghee
- 1 small onion, chopped
- 2 medium carrots, chopped
- ½ a pound of cremini mushrooms
- 3 garlic cloves, peeled and crushed
- 2 cups of 14-ounce cherry tomatoes
- ½ a cup of 2 ounces of pitted green olives
- ¼ teaspoon of freshly cracked black pepper
- ½ a cup of thinly sliced basil leaves
- ¼ a cup of coarsely chopped Italian parsley

Method:

1. Season the chicken thigh with ¾ teaspoon of kosher salt and keep it in your fridge for about 2 days

2. Set your Ninja Foodi to Saute mode and add ghee and allow it to melt

3. Once the Ghee is simmering, add carrots, onions, mushrooms and ½ a teaspoon of salt

4. Saute the veggies until they are tender (should be around 3-5 minutes)

5. Drop the tomato paste and garlic to your pot and cook for 30 seconds

6. Add seasoned chicken to the pot alongside olives and cherry tomatoes

7. Give everything a stir

8. Lock up the lid and cook for 7-10 minutes at HIGH pressure

9. Once done, allow the pressure to quick release

10. Stir in fresh herbs and enjoy!

Nutritional Values (Per Serving)

- Calories: 250
- Fat: 9g
- Saturated Fat: 2 g
- Carbohydrates: 4 g
- Fiber: 1 g
- Sodium: 916 mg
- Protein: 56 g

Deliciious Ginger Chicken

(Prepping time: 10 minutes\ Cooking time: 10 minutes |For 4 servings)

Ingredients

- 1 tablespoon rice vinegar
- 1 tablespoon Truvia
- 1 tablespoon garlic, minced
- 1 tablespoon fresh ginger, minced
- 1 tablespoon sesame oil
- 2 tablespoons soy sauce
- 1 and ½ pound boneless, skinless chicken thigh, cut into large pieces

Directions

1. Take a heatproof bowl and add soy sauce, ginger, sesame oil, garlic, Truvia, and vinegar

2. Stir well to coat it

3. Cover bowl with foil

4. Add 2 cups of water to Ninja Foodie's inner pot

5. Place a trivet and place the bowl with chicken on the trivet

6. Lock lid and cook for 10 minutes on HIGH pressure

7. Release pressure naturally over 10 minutes

8. Remove chicken and shred it, mix it back into the bowl

9. Serve and enjoy!

Nutrition Values (Per Serving)

- Calories: 118
- Fats: 10g
- Carbs: 7g
- Protein: 3g
- Sodium: 324g
- Fiber: 2g
- Saturated Fat: 3g

Fresh Pina Colada Chicken

Prep Time: 10 minutes

Cooking Time: 15 minutes

Number of Servings: 4

Ingredients:

- 2 pounds organic chicken thigh
- 1 cup fresh pineapple chunks
- ½ cup coconut cream
- 1 teaspoon cinnamon
- 1/8 teaspoon salt
- 2 tablespoons coconut aminos
- ½ cup green onion, chopped
- Arrowroot flout

Method:

1. Add listed ingredients to Ninja Foodi, except green onion

2. Lock lid and cook on HIGH pressure for 15 minutes

3. Release pressure naturally over 10 minutes

4. Open the lid and stir well

5. Take a bowl and mix in arrowroot, add tablespoon water and make a slurry

6. Add slurry to the pot and mix well

7. Set your pot to Saute mode and let it sit until the sauce is thick

8. Garnish with green onion and serve

9. Enjoy!

Nutritional Values (Per Serving)

- Calories: 358
- Fat: 20 g
- Saturated Fat: 4 g

- Carbohydrates: 8 g
- Fiber: 1 g
- Sodium: 1589 mg
- Protein: 12 g

Sesame Ginger Chicken

Prep Time: 10 minutes

Cooking Time: 10 minutes

Number of Servings: 4

Ingredients:

- 1 tablespoon rice vinegar
- 1 tablespoon Truvia
- 1 tablespoon garlic, minced
- 1 tablespoon fresh ginger, minced
- 1 tablespoon sesame oil
- 2 tablespoons soy sauce
- 1 and ½ pound boneless, skinless chicken thigh, cut into large pieces

Method:

1. Take a heatproof bowl and add soy sauce, ginger, sesame oil, garlic, Truvia and vinegar

2. Stir well to coat it

3. Cover bowl with foil

4. Add 2 cups of water to Ninja Foodie's inner pot

5. Place a trivet and place the bowl with chicken on the trivet

6. Lock lid and cook for 10 minutes on HIGH pressure

7. Release pressure naturally over 10 minutes

8. Remove chicken and shred it, mix it back into the bowl

9. Serve and enjoy!

Nutritional Values (Per Serving)

- Calories: 118
- Fat: 10 g
- Saturated Fat: 3 g
- Carbohydrates: 7 g

- Fiber: 2 g
- Sodium: 1280 mg
- Protein: 3 g

Mushroom And Chicken Bowl

Prep Time: 10 minutes

Cooking Time: 25 minutes

Number of Servings: 4

Ingredients:

- 1 and ½ cups unsweetened coconut milk
- 1 pound chicken thigh, skinless
- 3-4 garlic cloves, crushed
- ½ an onion, finely diced
- 2-inch knob ginger, minced
- 1 cup mushrooms, sliced
- 4 ounces baby spinach
- ½ teaspoon of cayenne pepper

- ½ teaspoon turmeric
- 1 teaspoon salt
- 1 teaspoon Garam Masala
- ¼ cup cilantro, chopped

Method:

1. Take your Ninja Foodi and add listed ingredients, stir well
2. Lock lid and cook on HIGH pressure for 15 minutes
3. Release pressure naturally over 10 minutes
4. Remove chicken, use an immersion blender to puree the vegetable
5. Shred chicken well and transfer it back to the pot
6. Add cream and gently stir
7. Serve and enjoy!

Nutritional Values (Per Serving)

- Calories: 289
- Fat:18 g
- Saturated Fat: 5 g
- Carbohydrates: 5 g
- Fiber: 2 g
- Sodium: 1844 mg
- Protein: 14 g

Spicy Poblano Chicken

Prep Time: 10 minutes

Cooking Time: 15 minutes

Number of Servings: 4

Ingredients:

- 1 cup onion, diced
- 3 poblano peppers, chopped
- 5 garlic cloves,1 cup cauliflower, diced
- 1 and ½ pounds large chicken breast chunks
- ¼ cup cilantro, chopped
- 1 teaspoon ground coriander
- 1 teaspoon ground cumin
- 1-2 teaspoons salt
- 2 and ½ cups of water
- 2 ounces cream cheese

Method:

1. Add listed ingredients except cheese to the Ninja Foodi

2. Lock lid and cook on HIGH pressure for 15 minutes

3. Release pressure naturally over 10 minutes

4. Remove chicken using tongs, keep it on the side

5. Blend the vegetables using an immersion blender

6. Set your pot to Saute mode

7. Let the broth heat up, add cream cheese, cut into chunks

8. Whisk well, reintroduce the shredded chicken back to the pot

9. Serve and enjoy!

Nutritional Values (Per Serving)

- Calories: 620
- Fat:47 g
- Saturated Fat: 10 g
- Carbohydrates: 14 g

- Fiber: 1 g
- Sodium: 413 mg
- Protein: 54 g

Chapter 4: Fish And Seafood Recipes

Awesome Sock-Eye Salmon

(Prepping time: 5 minutes\ Cooking time: 5 minutes |For 4 servings)

Ingredients

- 4 sockeye salmon fillets
- 1 teaspoon Dijon mustard
- ¼ teaspoon garlic, minced
- ¼ teaspoon onion powder
- ¼ teaspoon lemon pepper
- ½ teaspoon garlic powder
- ¼ teaspoon salt
- 2 tablespoons olive oil
- 1 and ½ cup of water

Directions

1. Take a bowl and add mustard, lemon juice, onion powder, lemon pepper, garlic powder, salt, olive oil

2. Brush spice mix over salmon

3. Add water to Instant Pot

4. Place rack and place salmon fillets on rack

5. Lock lid and cook on LOW pressure for 7 minutes

6. Quick-release pressure

7. Serve and enjoy!

Nutrition Values (Per Serving)

- Calories: 353
- Fat: 25g
- Carbohydrates: 0.6g
- Protein: 40g
- Sodium: 1400g
- Fiber: 0.1g
- Saturated Fat: 5g

Lovely Panko Cod

(Prepping time: 5 minutes\ Cooking time: 15 minutes |For 6 servings)

Ingredients

- 2 uncooked cod fillets, 6 ounces each
- 3 teaspoons kosher salt
- ¾ cup panko bread crumbs
- 2 tablespoons butter, melted
- ¼ cup fresh parsley, minced
- 1 lemon. Zested and juiced

Directions

1. Pre-heat your Ninja Foodi at 390 degrees F and place Air Crisper basket inside

2. Season cod and salt

3. Take a bowl and add bread crumbs, parsley, lemon juice, zest, butter, and mix well

4. Coat fillets with the bread crumbs mixture and place fillets in your Air Crisping basket

5. Lock Air Crisping lid and cook on Air Crisp mode for 15 minutes at 360 degrees F

6. Serve and enjoy!

Nutrition Values (Per Serving)

- Calories: 554
- Fat: 24g

- Carbohydrates: 5g
- Protein: 37g
- Sodium: 49g
- Fiber: 1g
- Saturated Fat: 5g

Buttery Salmon Fish

Prep Time: 10 minutes

Cooking Time: 30 minutes

Number of Servings: 4

Ingredients:

- 1 pound salmon fillets
- 2 tablespoons ginger/garlic paste
- 3 green chilies, chopped
- Salt and pepper to taste
- ¾ cup butter

Method:

1. Season salmon fillets with ginger, garlic paste, salt, pepper
2. Place salmon fillets to Ninja Foodi and top with green chilies and butter
3. Lock lid and BAKE/ROAST for 30 minutes at 360 degrees F
4. Bake for 30 minutes and enjoy!

Nutritional Values (Per Serving)

- Calories: 507
- Fat: 45g
- Saturated Fat: 8 g
- Carbohydrates: 3 g
- Fiber: 1 g
- Sodium: 762 mg
- Protein: 22 g

Cherry And Tomato Mackerel

Prep Time: 10 minutes

Cooking Time: 7 minutes

Number of Servings: 4

Ingredients:

- 4 Mackerel Fillets
- ¼ teaspoon onion powder
- ¼ teaspoon lemon powder
- ¼ teaspoon garlic powder
- ½ teaspoon salt
- 2 cups cherry tomatoes
- 3 tablespoons melted butter
- 1 and ½ cups of water
- 1 tablespoon black olives

Method:

1. Grease baking dish and arrange cherry tomatoes at the bottom of the dish

2. Top with fillets sprinkle all spices

3. Drizzle melted butter over

4. Add water to your Ninja Foodi

5. Lower rack in Ninja Foodi and place baking dish on top of the rack

6. Lock lid and cook on LOW pressure for 7 minutes

7. Quick-release pressure

8. Serve and enjoy!

Nutritional Values (Per Serving)

- Calories: 325
- Fat: 24g
- Saturated Fat: 3 g

- Carbohydrates: 2 g
- Fiber: 1 g
- Sodium: 0112mg
- Protein: 21 g

Juicy Seafood Stew

(Prepping time: 10 minutes\ Cooking time: 10 minutes |For 4 servings)

Ingredients

- 3 tablespoons extra virgin olive oil
- 2 bay leaves
- 2 teaspoons paprika
- 1 small onion, sliced
- 1 small green bell pepper
- 2 garlic cloves, mashed
- Salt and pepper to taste
- 1 cup fish stock
- 1 and ½ pound meat fish
- 1 pound shrimp, cleaned and deveined
- 12 neck clams
- ¼ cup cilantro, garnish
- 1 tablespoon extra virgin olive oil

Directions

1. Set your Ninja Foodi to Saute mode and add olive oil

2. Add bay leaves and paprika and Saute for 30 seconds

3. Add onion, bell pepper, tomatoes, 2 tablespoons of cilantro, garlic and season with salt and pepper

4. Stir for a few minutes

5. Add fish stock

6. Season fish with salt and pepper and Nestle the clams and shrimp among the veggies in the Ninja Foodi

7. Add fish on top

8. Lock up the lid and cook on HIGH pressure for 10 minutes

9. Release the pressure over 10 minutes

10. Divide the stew amongst bowls and drizzle 1 tablespoon of olive oil

11. Sprinkle 2 tablespoon of cilantro and serve

12. Enjoy!

Nutrition Values (Per Serving)

- Calories: 401
- Fats: 20g
- Carbs:9g
- Protein:41g
- Sodium: 741g
- Fiber: 3g
- Saturated Fat: 2g

Spicy Salmon Paprika

Prep Time: 10 minutes

Cooking Time: 7 minutes

Number of Servings: 4

Ingredients:

- 2 wild-caught salmon fillets, 1 to 1 and ½ inches thick
- 2 teaspoons avocado oil
- 2 teaspoons paprika
- Salt and pepper to taste
- Green herbs to garnish

Method:

1. Season salmon fillets with salt, pepper, paprika, and olive oil

2. Place Crisping basket in your Ninja Foodi, and pre-heat your Ninja Foodie at 390 degrees F

3. Place insert insider your Foodi and place the fillet in the insert, lock Air Crisping lid and cook for 7 minutes

4. Once done, serve the fish with herbs on top

5. Enjoy!

<u>Nutritional Values (Per Serving)</u>

- Calories: 246
- Fat: 11g
- Saturated Fat: 4 g
- Carbohydrates: 1.8 g
- Fiber: 2 g
- Sodium: mg
- Protein: 35 g

Hearty Cod Fillets

Prep Time: 10 minutes

Cooking Time: 5-10 minutes

Number of Servings: 4

Ingredients:

- 1 pound frozen codfish fillets
- 2 garlic cloves, halved
- 1 cup chicken broth
- ½ cup packed parsley
- 2 tablespoons oregano
- 2 tablespoons almonds, sliced½ teaspoon paprika

Method:

1. Take the fish out of the freezer and let it defrost

2. Take a food processor and stir in garlic, oregano, parsley, paprika, 1 tablespoon almond and process

3. Set your Ninja Foodi to "SAUTE" mode and add olive oil, let it heat up

4. Add remaining almonds and toast, transfer to a towel

5. Pour broth in a pot and add the herb mixture

6. Cut fish into 4 pieces and place in a steamer basket, transfer steamer basket to the pot

7. Lock lid and cook on HIGH pressure for 3 minutes

8. Quick-release pressure once has done

9. Serve steamed fish by pouring over the sauce

10. Enjoy!

Nutritional Values (Per Serving)

- Calories: 246
- Fat: 10g
- Saturated Fat: 3 g
- Carbohydrates: 8 g

- Fiber: 2 g
- Sodium: mg
- Protein: 15 g

Simple Salmon Stew

Prep Time: 10 minutes – 60 minutes

Cooking Time: 5-10 minutes

Number of Servings: 4

Ingredients:

- 1 cup fish broth
- Salt and pepper to taste
- 1 medium onion, chopped
- 1-2 pounds salmon fillets, cubed
- 1 tablespoon butter

Method:

1. Take a large-sized bowl and add shrimp, alongside listed ingredients

2. Let them sit for 30 -50 minutes

3. Take your inner pot and grease it well, add butter and transfer the marinated shrimp to the pot

4. Lock lid and cook on BAKE/ROAST mode for 15 minutes at 355 degrees F

5. Open the lid, serve, and enjoy!

Nutritional Values (Per Serving)

- Calories: 173
- Fat: 8g
- Saturated Fat: 2 g
- Carbohydrates: 0.1 g
- Fiber: 0 g
- Sodium: mg
- Protein: 23 g

Chapter 5: Beef And Lamb Recipes

Original Shepherds Pie

(Prepping time: 10 minutes\ Cooking time: 10-15 minutes |For 4 servings)

Ingredients

- 2 cups of water
- 4 tablespoons butter
- 4 ounces cream cheese
- 1 cup mozzarella
- 1 whole egg
- Salt and pepper to taste
- 1 tablespoon garlic powder
- 2-3 pounds ground beef
- 1 cup frozen carrots
- 8 ounces mushrooms, sliced
- 1 cup beef broth

Directions

1. Add water to Ninja Foodi, arrange cauliflower on top, lock lid and cook for 5 minutes on HIGH pressure

2. Quick-release and transfer to a blender; add cream cheese, butter, mozzarella cheese, egg, pepper, and salt. Blend well

3. Drain water from Ninja Foodi and add beef

4. Add carrots, garlic powder, broth and pepper, and salt

5. Add in cauliflower mix and lock lid, cook for 10 minutes on HIGH pressure

6. Release pressure naturally over 10 minutes

7. Serve and enjoy!

Nutrition Values (Per Serving)

- Calories: 303
- Fats: 21g
- Carbs: 4g
- Protein: 21g
- Sodium: 373g
- Fiber: 3g
- Saturated Fat: 1g

Korean Feisty Ribs

(Prepping time: 10 minutes\ Cooking time: 45 minutes |For 6 servings)

Ingredients

- 1 teaspoon olive oil
- 2 green onions, cut into 1-inch length
- 3 garlic cloves, smashed
- 3 quarter-sized ginger slices
- 4 pounds beef short ribs, 3 inches thick, cut into 3 rib portions
- ½ cup of water
- ½ cup coconut aminos
- ¼ cup dry white wine
- 2 teaspoons sesame oil
- Mince green onions for serving

Directions

1. Set your Ninja Foodi to "SAUTE" mode and add oil, let it shimmer

2. Add green onions, garlic, ginger, Saute for 1 minute

3. Add short ribs, water, amines, wine, sesame oil, and stir until the ribs are coated well

4. Lock lid and cook on HIGH pressure for 45 minutes

5. Release pressure naturally over 10 minutes

6. Remove short ribs from pot and serve with the cooking liquid

7. Enjoy!

Nutrition Values (Per Serving)

- Calories: 423
- Fat: 35g
- Carbohydrates: 4g
- Protein: 22g
- Sodium: 529g
- Fiber: 1g
- Saturated Fat: 7g

Butter Beef

(Prepping time: 5 minutes\ Cooking time: 60 minutes |For 6 servings)

Ingredients

- 3 pounds beef roast
- 1 tablespoon olive oil
- 2 tablespoons Keto-Friendly ranch dressing
- 1 jar pepper rings, with juices
- 8 tablespoons butter
- 1 cup of water

Directions

1. Set your Ninja Foodi to Saute mode and add 1 tablespoon of oil

2. Once the oil is hot, add roast and sear both sides

3. Set the Saute off and add water, seasoning mix, reserved juice, and pepper rings on top of your beef

4. Lock up the lid and cook on HIGH pressure for 60 minutes

5. Release the pressure naturally over 10 minutes

6. Cut the beef with salad sheers and serve with pureed cauliflower

7. Enjoy!

Nutrition Values (Per Serving)

- Calories: 269
- Fat: 18g

- Carbohydrates: 12g
- Protein: 16g
- Sodium: 1586g
- Fiber: 1g
- Saturated Fat: 4g

Short Braised Ribs

(Prepping time: 10 minutes\ Cooking time: 35 minutes |For 4 servings)

Ingredients

- 4 pounds beef short ribs
- A generous amount of kosher salt
- 1 tablespoon beef fat
- 1 onion, skin on, quartered
- 3 garlic cloves
- Water as needed

Directions

1. Season the ribs generously with salt

2. Take a skillet and heat the beef oil over medium-high. Toss in the ribs and gently cook them until browned

3. Once browned, toss in the garlic, onion, and about 2 inches of water.

4. Once mixed, transfer the mixture to the instant pot

5. Lock lid and cook on HIGH pressure for 35 minutes

6. Release pressure naturally over 10 minutes

7. Once the ribs complete, serve the dish with the dish on the bone

8. Alternatively, you can also pull the meat from the bones and braise the liquid and skim the fat. Store them in a jar and serve the ribs with the broth making sure to season them well.

<u>Nutrition Values (Per Serving)</u>

- Calories: 308
- Fat: 18g
- Carbohydrates: 5g
- Protein: 31g
- Sodium: 381g
- Fiber: 2g
- Saturated Fat: 2g

Tender Pineapple Flavored Steak

Prep Time: 5-10 minutes

Cooking Time: 8 minutes

Number of Servings: 4

Ingredients:

- ½ medium pineapple, cored and diced
- 1 jalapeno, seeded and stemmed, diced
- 1 medium red onion, diced
- 4 pieces filet mignon steaks, 6-8 ounces each
- 1 tablespoon canola oil
- Salt and pepper to taste
- 1 tablespoon lime juice
- ¼ cup cilantro leaves, chopped
- Chili powder and ground coriander

Method:

1. Rub fillets with oil evenly, season them well with salt and pepper
2. Pre-heat Ninja Foodi by pressing the "GRILL" option and setting it to "HIGH" and timer to 8 minutes
3. Let it pre-heat until you hear a beep
4. Arrange fillets over grill grate, lock lid and cook for 4 minutes until the internal temperature reaches 125 degrees F
5. Take a mixing bowl and add pineapple, onion, jalapeno, mix well
6. Add lime juice, cilantro, chili powder, coriander and combine
7. Serve fillets with the pineapple mixture on top
8. Enjoy!

Nutritional Values (Per Serving)

- Calories: 530
- Fat: 22 g
- Saturated Fat: 7 g

- Carbohydrates: 21 g
- Fiber: 4 g
- Sodium: 286 mg
- Protein: 58 g

Coffee Flavored Steak

Prep Time: 10 minutes

Cooking Time: 50 minutes

Number of Servings: 4

Ingredients:

- 1 and ½ pounds beef flank steak
- 1 teaspoon instant espresso powder
- ½ teaspoon garlic powder
- 2 teaspoons chili powder
- 2 tablespoons olive oil
- Salt and pepper, to taste

Method:

1. Insert the grill grate and close the hood
2. Pre-heat Ninja Foodi by pressing the "GRILL" option at and setting it to "HIGH" and timer to 40 minutes
3. Once it pre-heat until you hear a beep
4. Make the dry rub by mixing the chili powder, espresso powder, garlic powder, salt, and pepper
5. Rub all over the steak and brush with oil
6. Place on the grill grate and cook for 40 minutes
7. Flip after 20 minutes
8. Serve and enjoy!

<u>Nutritional Values (Per Serving)</u>

- Calories: 250
- Fat: 14 g
- Saturated Fat: 4 g
- Carbohydrates: 6 g
- Fiber: 2 g
- Sodium: 294 mg
- Protein: 20 g

Easy Going Avocado And Beef Dish

Prep Time: 5-10 minutes

Cooking Time: 18 minutes

Number of Servings: 4

Ingredients:

- 1 cup cilantro leaves
- 2 ripe avocados, diced
- 2 cups salsa Verde
- 2 beef flank steak, diced
- ½ teaspoon salt
- ½ teaspoon pepper
- 2 medium tomatoes, seeded and diced

Method:

1. Rub beef steak with salt and pepper, season well

2. Pre-heat Ninja Foodi by pressing the "GRILL" option and setting it to "MED" and timer to 18 minutes

3. Let it pre-heat until you hear a beep

4. Arrange diced steak over grill grate, lock lid and cook for 9 minutes

5. Flip and cook for 9 minutes more

6. Take a blender and blend in salsa, cilantro

7. Serve with grilled steak, with blended salsa, tomato, and avocado

8. Enjoy!

Nutritional Values (Per Serving)

- Calories: 520
- Fat: 31 g
- Saturated Fat: 9 g
- Carbohydrates: 38 g
- Fiber: 2 g
- Sodium: 301 mg
- Protein: 41 g

Mexican Beef Delight

(Prepping time: 5 minutes\ Cooking time: 12 minutes |For 4 servings)

Ingredients

- 2 and ½ pounds boneless beef short ribs
- 1 tablespoon chili powder
- 1 and ½ teaspoons salt
- 1 tablespoon fat
- 1 medium onion, thinly sliced
- 1 tablespoon tomato sauce
- 6 garlic cloves, peeled and smashed
- ½ cup roasted tomato salsa
- ½ cup bone broth
- Fresh ground black pepper
- ½ cup cilantro, minced
- 2 radishes, sliced

Directions

1. Take a large-sized bowl and add the cubed beef, salt, and chili powder; give it a nice mix

2. Set your Ninja Foodi to Saute mode and add butter, allow it to melt

3. Add garlic and tomato paste and Saute for 30 seconds

4. Add seasoned beef, stock, and fish sauce

5. Lock up the lid and cook on HIGH pressure for 35 minutes on MEAT/STEW mode

6. Release the pressure naturally over 10 minutes

7. Season with some salt and pepper and enjoy!

Nutrition Values (Per Serving)

- Calories: 308
- Fats: 18g
- Carbs:21g
- Protein:38g
- Sodium: 737g
- Fiber: 3g
- Saturated Fat: 5g

Lovely Goulash

(Prepping time: 10 minutes\ Cooking time: 15-20 minutes |For 4 servings)

Ingredients

- 1-2 pounds extra lean beef, ground
- 2 teaspoons olive oil + 11 teaspoons extra
- 1 large red bell pepper, stemmed and seeded
- 1 large onion, cut into short strips
- 1 tablespoon garlic, minced
- 2 tablespoons sweet paprika
- ½ teaspoon hot paprika
- 4 cups beef stock
- 2 cans tomatoes, diced and petite

Directions

1. Set your Ninja Foodi to Saute mode and add 2 teaspoons of olive oil

2. Add ground beef to the pot and cook, making sure to stir it until it breaks apart

3. Once the beef is browned, transfer it to a bowl

4. Cut the steam off the pepper and deseed them and cut into strips

5. Cut the onion into short strips as well

6. Add a teaspoon of olive oil to the pot alongside pepper and onion

7. Saute for 3-4 minutes

8. Add minced garlic, sweet paprika, hot paprika and cook for 2-3 minutes

9. Add beef stock alongside the tomatoes

10. Add ground beef

11. Allow it to cook for about 15 minutes on Soup mode over the low pressure

12. Once done, quickly release the pressure and have fun!

Nutrition Values (Per Serving)

- Calories: 213
- Fat: 9g
- Carbohydrates: 2g
- Protein: 26g
- Sodium: 612g
- Fiber: 0g
- Saturated Fat: 3g

Beef And Broccoli Delight

(Prepping time: 5 minutes\ Cooking time:6-8 hours |For 6 servings)

Ingredients

- 1 and ½ pounds beef round steak, cut into 2 inches by 1/8 inch strips
- 1 cup broccoli, diced
- ½ teaspoon red pepper flakes
- 2 teaspoon garlic, minced
- 2 teaspoons olive oil
- 2 tablespoons apple cider vinegar
- 2 tablespoons coconut aminos
- 2 tablespoons white wine vinegar
- 1 tablespoons arrowroot
- ¼ cup beef broth

Directions

1. Take a large-sized bowl and make the sauce by mixing in red pepper flakes, olive oil, coconut aminos, garlic, white wine vinegar, apple cider vinegar, broth, and arrowroot

2. Mix well

3. Add the mix to your Ninja Foodi

4. Add beef and place a lid

5. Cook on SLOW COOK MODE (LOW) for 6-8 hours

6. Uncover just 30 minutes before end time and add broccoli, lock lid again and let it finish

7. Serve and enjoy!

Nutrition Values (Per Serving)

- Calories: 208
- Fat: 12g
- Carbohydrates: 11g
- Protein: 15g
- Sodium: 973g
- Fiber: 3g
- Saturated Fat: 3g

Favorite Party Lamb Gyros

(Prepping time: 10 minutes\ Cooking time: 25 minutes |For 8 servings)

Ingredients

- 8 garlic cloves
- 1 and ½ teaspoon salt
- 2 teaspoons dried oregano
- 1 and ½ cups of water
- 2 pounds lamb meat, ground
- 2 teaspoons rosemary
- ½ teaspoon pepper
- 1 small onion, chopped
- 2 teaspoons ground marjoram

Directions

1. Add onions, garlic, marjoram, rosemary, salt, and pepper to a food processor

2. Process until combined well, add ground lamb meat and process again

3. Press meat mixture gently into a loaf pan

4. Transfer the pan to your Ninja Foodi pot

5. Lock lid and select "Bake/Roast" mode

6. Bake for 25 minutes at 375 degrees F

7. Transfer to serving the dish and enjoy it!

Nutrition Values (Per Serving)

- Calories: 242

- Fat: 15g

- Carbohydrates: 2.4g

- Protein: 21g

- Sodium: 585g

- Fiber: 1g

- Saturated Fat: 3g

Chapter 6: Snacks And Appetizers

Warm Egg Frittata

(Prepping time: 10 minutes \ Cooking time: 15 minutes |For 4 servings)

Ingredients

- 5 whole eggs
- ¾ teaspoon mixed herbs
- 1 cup spinach
- ¼ cup shredded cheddar cheese
- ½ cup mushrooms
- Salt and pepper to taste

  ¾ cup half and half

  2 tablespoons butter

Directions

1. Dice mushrooms, chop spinach finely

2. Set your Ninja Foodi to Saute mode and add spinach, mushrooms

3. Whisk eggs, milk, cream cheese, herbs, and Sautéed vegetables in a bowl and mix well

4. Take a 6-inch baking pan and grease it well

5. Pour mixture and transfer to your Ninja Foodie (on a trivet)

6. Cook on HIGH pressure for 2 minutes

7. Quick-release pressure

8. Serve and enjoy!

Nutrition Values (Per Serving)

- Calories: 300
- Fat: 25g
- Carbohydrates: 5g
- Protein: 14g
- Sodium: 255g
- Fiber: 2g
- Saturated Fat: 5g

Egg Dredged Casserole

(Prepping time: 10 minutes\ Cooking time: 5 minutes |For 6 servings)

Ingredients

- 4 whole eggs
- 1 tablespoons milk
- 1 tomato, diced
- ½ cup spinach
- ¼ teaspoon salt
- ¼ teaspoon ground black pepper

Directions

1. Take a baking pan (small enough to fit Ninja Foodi) and grease it with butter

2. Take a medium bowl and whisk in eggs, milk, salt, pepper, add veggies to the bowl and stir

3. Pour egg mixture into the baking pan and lower the pan into the Ninja Foodi

4. Close Air Crisping lid and Air Crisp for 325 degrees for 7 minutes

5. Remove the pan from eggs, and enjoy hot!

Nutrition Values (Per Serving)

- Calories: 78
- Fat: 5g
- Carbohydrates: 1g
- Protein: 7g

- Sodium: 528g
- Fiber: 0g
- Saturated Fat: 2g

Rosemary Flavored Potatoes

Prep Time: 10 minutes

Cooking Time: 20 minutes

Number of Servings: 4

Ingredients:

- 2 pounds baby red potatoes, quartered
- 2 tablespoons extra virgin olive oil
- ¼ cup dried onion flakes
- ½ teaspoon onion powder
- ½ teaspoon garlic powder
- ¼ teaspoon celery powder
- ¼ teaspoon freshly ground black pepper
- ½ teaspoon dried parsley
- ½ teaspoon salt

Method:

1. Take a large bowl and add all listed ingredients, toss well and coat them well

2. Pre-heat Ninja Foodi by pressing the "AIR CRISP" option and setting it to "390 Degrees F" and timer to 20 minutes

3. let it pre-heat until you hear a beep

4. Once preheated, add potatoes to the cooking basket

5. Lock and cook for 10 minutes, making sure to shake the basket and cook for 10 minutes more

6. Once done, check the crispiness, if it's alright, serve away.

7. If not, cook for 5 minutes more

8. Enjoy!

<u>Nutritional Values (Per Serving)</u>

- Calories: 232

- Fat: 7 g
- Saturated Fat: 1 g
- Carbohydrates: 39 g
- Fiber: 6 g
- Sodium: 249 mg
- Protein: 4 g

Homely Honey Flavored Asparagus

Prep Time: 5-10 minutes

Cooking Time: 15 minutes

Number of Servings: 4

Ingredients:

- 2 pounds asparagus, trimmed
- ½ teaspoon pepper
- 1 teaspoon salt
- ¼ cup honey
- 2 tablespoons olive oil
- 4 tablespoons tarragon, minced

Method:

1. Take a bowl and add asparagus, oil, salt, honey, pepper, tarragon and toss well

2. Pre-heat Ninja Foodi by pressing the "GRILL" option and setting it to "MED" and timer to 8 minutes

3. Let it pre-heat until you hear a beep

4. Arrange asparagus over grill grate, lock lid and cook for 4 minutes, flip asparagus and cook for 4 minutes more

5. Serve and enjoy!

<u>Nutritional Values (Per Serving)</u>

- Calories: 240
- Fat: 15 g
- Saturated Fat: 3 g
- Carbohydrates: 31 g
- Fiber: 1 g
- Sodium: 103 mg
- Protein: 7 g

Subtle Italian Squash

Prep Time: 5-10 minutes

Cooking Time: 16 minutes

Number of Servings: 4

Ingredients:

- 1 medium butternut squash, peeled, seeded and cut into ½ inch slices
- 1 teaspoon dried thyme
- ½ teaspoon salt
- 1 tablespoon olive oil
- 1 and ½ teaspoons dried oregano
- ¼ teaspoon black pepper

Method:

1. Take a mixing bowl and add slices alongside other ingredients, mix well

2. Pre-heat Ninja Foodi by pressing the "GRILL" option and setting it to "MED" and timer to 16 minutes

3. let it pre-heat until you hear a beep

4. Arrange squash slices over the grill grate

5. Cook for 8 minutes, flip and cook for 8 minutes more

6. Serve and enjoy!

Nutritional Values (Per Serving)

- Calories: 238
- Fat: 12 g
- Saturated Fat: 2 g
- Carbohydrates: 36 g
- Fiber: 3 g
- Sodium: 128 mg
- Protein: 15 g

Printed in Great Britain
by Amazon